# Dear Parent:

## Your child's love of reading starts here!

Every child learns to read in a different way and at his or her own speed. Some go back and forth between reading levels and read favorite books again and again. Others read through each level in order. You can help your young reader improve and become more confident by encouraging his or her own interests and abilities. From books your child reads with you to the first books he or she reads alone, there are I Can Read Books for every stage of reading:

### SHARED READING
Basic language, word repetition, and whimsical illustrations, ideal for sharing with your emergent reader

### BEGINNING READING
Short sentences, familiar words, and simple concepts for children eager to read on their own

### READING WITH HELP
Engaging stories, longer sentences, and language play for developing readers

### READING ALONE
Complex plots, challenging vocabulary, and high-interest topics for the independent reader

I Can Read Books have introduced children to the joy of reading since 1957. Featuring award-winning authors and illustrators and a fabulous cast of beloved characters, I Can Read Books set the standard for beginning readers.

A lifetime of discovery begins with the magical words "I Can Read!"

*Visit www.icanread.com for information on enriching your child's reading experience.*

*For Señorita Marselli*
*(aka Señora LaRosa)*
*—L.D.*

*To all the teachers who*
*selflessly invest in the*
*future generations*
*—C.E.*

I Can Read® and I Can Read Book® are trademarks of HarperCollins Publishers.
I Want to Be a Teacher
Copyright © 2021 by HarperCollins Publishers
All rights reserved. Printed in the United States of America. No part of this book may be used or reproduced in any manner whatsoever without written permission except in the case of brief quotations embodied in critical articles and reviews. For information address HarperCollins Children's Books, a division of HarperCollins Publishers, 195 Broadway, New York, NY 10007.
www.icanread.com

Library of Congress Control Number: 2020942482
ISBN 978-0-06-298955-0 (trade bdg.) — ISBN 978-0-06-298954-3 (pbk.)

21 22 23 24  LSCC  10 9 8 7 6 5 4 3 2  ❖  First Edition

# I Want to Be a
# Teacher

by Laura Driscoll
pictures by Catalina Echeverri

**HARPER**
*An Imprint of HarperCollinsPublishers*

My sister Stella
is learning to talk!
I am teaching her
some words.

"Can you say 'Mama'?" I ask her.

"Ma ma," says Stella.

"Can you say 'Dada'?"

I ask Stella.

"Da da," Stella says.

Dad smiles.

"You are a good teacher,"

Dad says to me.

I have taught Stella to say "bye bye."

I have taught Stella to say "no."

She can even say

our sister's name—Lucy.

"Ooo see," says Stella.

I point to myself.

"Can you say 'Noah'?" I ask.

Stella stuffs cereal
into her mouth.

I try again.

"No. Aaah. Noah." I say.

Stella is done talking.

I want Stella to learn my name!

"We will try again later," I tell her.

It is time for me

to go see my own teachers.

I know a lot of teachers.

Miss Finch is my school teacher.

In our classroom,
Miss Finch teaches us
to read new words.

Miss Finch teaches us
about important people.

Miss Finch teaches us

how to be a good friend.

Some days,

I go down the hall

to Ms. Foy's room.

She is my speech teacher.

I repeat after Ms. Foy.

"The rabbit is out in the rain," I say.

My R sounds are getting better!

On other days,

our class goes to the art room.

Mr. Case is teaching us

about the color wheel.

Did you know that

red and yellow makes orange?

Our gym teacher, Ms. Finn, shows us how to play blob tag at recess.

It is so tiring.

And so fun!

"You have to use teamwork

for this game!" Ms. Finn tells us.

At home, I get a snack.
My sister is at the table
with her math tutor, Jen.

Jen knows lots of cool tricks
for adding big numbers.

In the living room,

Mom is having her tuba lesson.

Her tuba teacher comes once a week.

"How do I sound?" Mom asks.

I give Mom a thumbs-up.

She is not perfect.

But she is way better

than when she started!

After dinner,

Dad takes me to my swim lesson.

My swim teacher, Tim, teaches me

arm strokes and bubble blowing.

At the end of the lesson,

I swim across the whole pool.

"I knew you could do it!" Tim says.

The next day is Saturday.

Mom takes Stella, Lucy,

Rocket, and me

to meet another teacher.

Dan is a dog trainer.

"A teacher for Rocket!"

I say.

Dan nods and adds,

"I will also teach you

how to teach Rocket."

One thing Dan teaches us
is not to let Rocket
eat off the table.

"Hear that, Stella?" I say.

"You have to say

'No, Rocket.'"

"No," says Stella.

She shakes her head.

Then Stella grins
and points at me.
"No," Stella says, "aaah.
No aaah."
NOAH!

Stella can say my name!

"You did it, Stella!" I say.

I am so proud of her.

It feels good to be a teacher!

# Meet the Teachers

### Classroom teacher
A teacher who works in a school and helps students learn and grow

### Speech teacher
A teacher who helps students make sounds correctly and speak more clearly

### Art teacher
A teacher who helps students make art—with drawing, coloring, painting, and more

### Gym teacher
A teacher who teaches games and sports to help students learn about health, fitness, cooperation, and playing fair

### Tutor
Someone who works one-on-one with a student to give extra help on schoolwork

### Music teacher
A teacher who leads a music class at a school or gives instrument lessons

### Swim instructor
A person trained to teach swim skills at a pool

### Animal trainer
An animal coach who can teach animals to behave in a certain way and can teac humans how to train their own pets